TRACTION & ROLLING STOCK ADVERTISER

An Introduction to

BRITISH INDUSTRIAL DIESEL LOCOMOTIVES

(standard gauge)

by

RAY KING

© Ray King 2006

First published in Great Britain 2006
by Barkers Publishing
on behalf of Traction & Rolling Stock Advertiser
82 Louies Lane Diss
Norfolk IP22 4QN
01379 651683

Printed in England by
Barkers Print & Design Ltd, Attleborough Norfolk NR17 2NP

INTRODUCTION

Over the years, books and films have been produced about many types of railway locomotive, from main line steam, diesel and electric, to specials and experimental ones. Industrial steam has also received plenty of coverage, both standard and narrow gauge. Most books on diesel shunters however only deal with those used by British Railways, or about a particular manufacturer. One area which is rarely covered is the industrial Diesel locomotive. A great variety of these vehicles were produced from many different manufacturers and today most railways still have a few. This book is designed to give an insight to the British Industrial Diesel Shunting Locomotives (standard gauge). Many people believe that 1950s to the 1970s was the heyday of the industrial diesel. Most were British built from a variety of manufacturers, with a few imports, mainly from the USA.

I have been involved with these machines for over 25 years, both as owner, maintainer and operator. My introduction was during a search for an economical locomotive and the first motive power for the fledgling Mid-Norfolk Railway. This search led me to the British Sugar Corporation at Bury St Edmunds, where I obtained a relatively new locomotive in full working order for a little over scrap price. I still use this locomotive on a regular basis at Bressingham Steam Museum, where it has shunted vehicles such as Oliver Cromwell and Green Arrow on their very steep line. I have found these vehicles easy to operate and maintain, as well as being perfectly able to perform most duties asked of them. I have deliberately chosen photos that show the varied work performed by these vehicles and tried to avoid many of the traditional three quarter views in sidings out of use. I have only scratched the surface in terms of the variety, but to show one of every type was not the objective, rather to show as many as possible in good or appropriate surroundings. I hope that the photographs in this book show these vehicles in a good light and the reader looks further into the subject and finds it as interesting as I do.

> Ray King, Diss 2006

In this book we look at standard gauge, but it must also be remembered in industry there were huge numbers of narrow gauge locomotives, mainly used in mines, quarries and construction projects. Today some systems still exist and can be found underground and on special construction projects like the Channel Tunnel.

Below.
Hudswell Clarke ex Port of Bristol Authority No 31 (HC D1172 of 1959) at Stroud coal wharf in 1979.

CONTENTS

Introduction . . . . Page 1

Contents . . . . Page 3

Industrial Railways . . . . Page 4

Diesel Replaces Steam . . . . Page 6

How it Works . . . . Page 7

Locomotive Photos

Locomotive Builders . . . . Page 50

Makers Plates & Emblems . . . . Page 54

Present Day . . . . Page 57

All photos are by the author except where shown.

Reference books used,
 "Industrial Locomotives" by The Industrial Railway Society.
 "Brush Diesel Locomotives 1940-78" by George Toms.
 "Barclay 150" by Russell Wear.
 "The Hunslet Engine Works" by D.H.Townsley.
 "Bagnall Locomotives" by Allan.C.Baker & T D Allen Civil.
 "Industrial Diesels" by A.J. Booth.
 "The Railways of the Manchester Ship Canal" by Don Thorpe.
 "G.E.C Traction and its predecessors - 1823 to the present day" by Rodger.P.Bradley.

plus, a great deal of help from people in the heritage railway movement, heritage railway web sites and stock books including;
Paul Appleby and **www.rail-photos.com**
www.preservedshunters.co.uk
Chris Fisher of Industrial Railway Society.
Alastair Baker.

Notes

Each photograph has details about the locomotive, i.e. HC D1234 of 1960.
Built by Hudswell Clarke & Co as No D1234 in 1960.
This is the build number given when made and will remain throughout its life,
unlike a fleet number given by the owner.

0-4-0 indicated that the wheels are externally coupled with rods.
4w indicates that it is internally coupled by chain.
Industrial diesels locomotives do not have un-powered carrying wheels.
DH, DE, DM indicate the transmission type, i.e. DE indicates a diesel engine driving
through a electric generator, DH is Hydraulic and DM is Mechanical.
TE, stands for Tractive Effort and is the pulling power exerted at the rails, normally expressed in lbs.

BAOR = British Army of the Rhine	BHP = Brake Horse Power
BNFL = British Nuclear Fuels Ltd.	BR = British Railways
BTH = British Thomson Houston Ltd.	Cyl = Cylinders.
CEGB = Central Electric Generating Board.	GEC = General Electric Company
GER = Great Eastern Railway	GET = Great Eastern Traction
GWR = Great Western Railway	IRS = Industrial Railway Society
LMS = London Midland & Scottish Railway	NCB = National Coal Board
MoD = Ministry of Defence	PW = Permanent Way
SRPS = Scottish Railway Preservation Society	

INDUSTRIAL RAILWAYS

Railways started to be developed when industry found the need to transport such things as coal, slate, and stone from the hills to the ports for transportation around the world. The lanes to the sea soon became very muddy and rutted, causing great problems for the mine owners. The solution was to lay stones and later wood or iron wheel supports. These were called plateways, later becoming railways. Wagons on these early plateways were in the main horse drawn, with some help from winding engines or gravity depending on the direction of travel. Locomotives started to replace horses in the early 1800s and developed very rapidly over the next 50 years. As the railways developed, different types of locomotives were required for different operations. The type of locomotives required to haul a fast passenger train between cities was different to the ones required to work within a factory or a quarry. Industrial locos differ from main line ones in a number of respects. Main line locos are generally required to go fast in a mainly straight line for long periods of time. Within industry it is necessary to continually go in different directions, shunting wagons and working in restricted locations, very often with poor adhesion/rail head conditions (mud or oil on the rail causing poor adhesion). Also because they are used in places where men are working, visibility is a top requirement. Some were fitted with a crane for working in shipyards, some were fireless (using steam from a static plant) for working in fire sensitive areas and some were built low for working in restricted locations. It called for short wheel base machines with good visibility and the ability to work just as well backwards as forwards, high speed was not a necessity. With the great diversity of environments in which they worked and with many different industries, variety increased. Yet they all had one thing in common, they used steam in their cylinders and coal for their boilers. In the early 1900s a new type of locomotive was starting to appear in shunting yards in the UK. The first internal combustion locomotives were petrol and started to appear in isolated locations from the early 1900s. One of the early applications was in the battlefields of WW1, where a cloud of steam would have given away the troops position, so petrol seemed an ideal solution. Diesel engines were introduced from about 1929.

Above. Carts similar to this one would have been used on early plateways, hauled by horses down to the docks. This reconstruction is at the Causey Arch near the Tanfield Railway in Co Durham, which claims to be the worlds oldest surviving working railway, having been in use since 1725. The Tanfield Railway itself is home to some very early diesel shunting locomotives and well worth a visit.

ndustrial railways were at one time a very common sight in the UK and their locomotives used very much s the modern lorry or tractor is today. It may be hard to realise how large some of the industrial systems vere. British Steel of Corby had at one time about 50 locomotives on site and they were not alone. Other arge users apart from the steel companies were the National Coal Board who still had well over 1,000 ocomotives in the 1970s. Others users were, MoD, British Sugar, Manchester Ship Canal, Port of Bristol, Mersey Docks & Harbour Board, Pilkingtons Glass etc etc. To give an idea of how large some of the ndustrial systems were we can look at the Manchester Ship Canal system. Manchester is a large city some 0 miles from the nearest shipping port. So in the late 1800s a large ship canal was constructed to allow eagoing vessels to travel from the River Mersey right into the heart of Manchester. A railway was built or its entire length, originally for the construction and later for servicing both the canal and the many firms hat sprang up along its length. At its height it had a total rail length of 230 miles and operated 75 ocomotives. When diesels were introduced between 1959 and 1966, over thirty locomotives were urchased from Hudswell Clarke & Co and later from Sentinel of Shrewsbury. Repairs and complete verhauls were handled by the docks own staff in a number of workshops along the system, the biggest eing at Mode Wheel. Today things have changed greatly with shipping traffic having ceased and most of he railway removed, but there are still two of the 1965 built RR Sentinels at the Barton Dock site.

Above. One of the larger systems was at British Steel in Corby. At times they had up to 50 locomotives vorking in the steel works and the associated quarries. In this photo taken in May 1975 four locos can be een including 0-6-0 diesel hydraulic D16 (EE D1049 of 1965) and D11 (EE D913 of 1964).

DIESEL REPLACES STEAM

In about 1930 a number of firms started to experiment with the new type of internal combustion engi
called the Diesel, named after Dr Rudolph Diesel. But it must be remembered that a British inventor Jan
Akroyd Stuart produced a compression ignition engine before Dr Diesel. From 1930 to about 19
progress was slow with steam still king, remember that British Railways was still making stea
locomotives up until 1960. Most firms carried on building steam, but some also started to produce a ran
of diesels as an alternative. The big four railway companies experimented in the mid 1930s with a fe
diesel shunters from a variety of manufacturers. They purchased small batches of different types
compare designs, engines and transmissions. They seemed successful, but there was still a great reluctar
to dispense with steam. A number of manufacturers that had not previously been known as locomoti
builders came to the new market such as Ruston, English Electric and Brush. On the whole these new fir
were very successful, with the last two mentioned becoming the major suppliers to BR. The new die
locomotives could easily do the work of three steam locomotives and with many other savings. A stea
locomotive needed hours to get up steam and two men to operate it, plus much fire cleaning, oiling a
boiler wash outs every few weeks. Also the requirement to fill up with water a number of times per d
and coaling at the end of each day. The diesel was ready with a push of a button and would happily wo
away from its maintenance facility for a week. The other big advantage was the vastly clear
environment, especially with many of the duties being within built up areas and near homes.

Below.
An idea of the improved visibility is given by this photo from inside Hunslet 0-4-0DH "ALLINGTC
CASTLE" (HE 6975 of 1968) at Medway Port in Kent. The easy controls and better driving environme
is also evident.

HOW IT WORKS

Construction.

British shunting locomotives were normally of the 4 or 6 wheeled variety, either rod drive 0-6-0/0-4-0 or chain drive 6w/4w. There were a few using bogie construction, Bo-Bo and in one case a Co-Co. Because of the harsh environment in which many worked the frames/chassis were made of very thick plate steel, in some cases buffer beams would be as much as 8" to 10" thick. Other features that make Industrial diesels stand out from the rest is that most have a radiator at the front, similar to a tractor and a trade name or logo on the front over the radiator grill. Some firms also had interesting badges and logos. They mostly all had a single cab with good all round vision making shunting easier and safer.

Engine.

Steam is an external combustion engine, where the fuel (coal or oil etc) is burned in a separate boiler and then fed into the cylinders (or engine) in measured amounts to move the cylinders at a required speed. Petrol and diesel engines are internal combustion engines, where the fuel is burnt in the cylinder and to change speed or power the amount of fuel is controlled. The advantages with the latter over steam is that power is instantly available and a fireman is not required, an accelerator automatically adjusts the fuel supply to the vehicles requirement. A disadvantage is that unlike a steam engine it requires a refined product and clean conditions. So for countries with large coal or wood stocks and no oil, steam held on much longer. The diesel/oil engine, or to give its correct name the compression ignition engine, differs from the familiar petrol engine in one fundamental respect. The burning process is caused by air being compressed in a cylinder and then a very fine spray of fuel oil is sprayed in at a designated point in the engine cycle, thus causing an explosion or rapid burning and forcing the piston to move. With petrol (spark ignition) engines, a mixture of petrol and air is fed into the engine and then a spark applied at the required moment. Diesel engines are much heavier than petrol and noisier because of the higher compression ratio needed to cause ignition, but they are much safer, as diesel is far less flammable that petrol. On a steam engine, full power is available from stationary, but on a internal combustion engine it has to be running at a reasonable speed to keep the ignition cycle going and to develop power. This means with a diesel locomotive we need a transmission system and gearbox.

Below. A typical layout for a diesel hydraulic or mechanical shunter with the radiator at the front followed by the engine, transmission and the final drive.

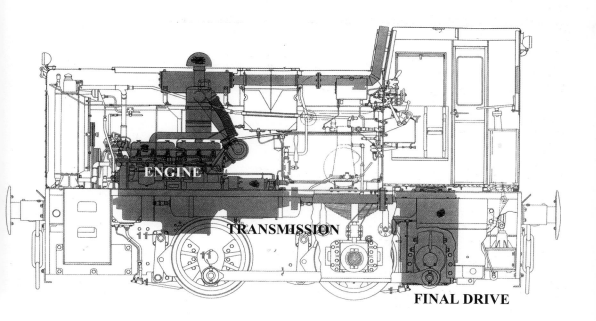

Transmission

There are three main types of transmission used on shunters, mechanical, hydraulic and electric. The earl[y] locomotives used mechanical transmission, with gears operated by levers similar to cars, but of cours[e] much heavier. These proved difficult to drive especially as shunters became larger, so a semi automati[c] gearbox became very popular. This was the Wilson Epicyclic gearbox made by Self Changing Gears [of] Coventry. This used a series of sun and planet gears together with brake bands to give a smooth ge[ar] change and very little effort on the part of the Driver. This was used together with a fluid flywheel, th[us] avoiding the need for a heavy clutch. Another form of transmission that proved very popular with shunt[er] owners was the hydraulic type. A number of variations were in use, but two of the favoured types we[re] Voith and Twin Disc. Voith was developed in Germany and also made in the UK under licence by the Nor[th] British Locomotive Company. It was also used in main line locos and some modern rail cars. The Tw[in] Disc was produced in the UK under US patent and proved very popular, giving very few problems. Th[e] third type was the electric transmission, tending to be used on the larger shunters and employed many par[ts] similar to main line locos. A generator was attached to the diesel engine and a traction motor connected [to] the axle, normally directly. Ruston used a electric motor mounted directly onto the final drive whic[h] removed the water sensitive motor high up in the chassis.

Final drive gearbox

With the mechanical and hydraulic transmission, due to the speed of the engine it is necessary to use [a] reduction gearbox to get the required tractive effort from a relatively small engine. This gearbox als[o] contained the reverse gears, as a railway locomotive, unlike other forms of motive power is required [to] travel at the same speed in reverse as in forward. The electric transmission does not require this gearbo[x] as the motor is normally fixed directly onto the axle and reverse is obtained by changing the direction [of] the electric current.

Brakes

Most industrial locomotives were fitted from new with air operated brakes that worked on the vehic[le] itself, using its weight to stop the wagons. This was fine in a small yard and gave them the tradition[al] sound of the clank, clank associated with such locations. Shunters built for BR mostly all had vacuu[m] brakes fitted as well, to operate the train brakes. As vacuum brakes gave way to air brakes all BR shunte[rs] and many industrial ones have been retrospectively fitted with air train brake equipment, often requirin[g] an additional large compressor to be fitted to give the required capacity.

Below. The Manchester firm of L Gardner & Sons Ltd was a major supplier for many early diesels a[nd] their products were well regarded. Seen here is the 8 Cylinder L3 type which can still be found in ma[ny] locos today.

Sir W.G.Armstrong Whitworth & Co were pioneers in diesel traction and built a number of diesel shunters using electric transmission from about 1930. Two survive from a batch of six built in 1933. Originally powered by a 6cyl Armstrong-Saunders 85bhp engine, driving Laurence Scott electrical equipment and weighing in at 15 tons.

Left. No 2 (AW D22 of 1933) is seen on the Marley Hill crossing at the Tanfield Railway in Durham. ***Photo by M Pearce of the Tanfield Railway.***

Inset.
(AW D21) is part of the National Collection and is seen at York.

Below. Bagnall of Stafford were a builder of steam locomotives from the 1870s who successfully branched into diesel production in the 1950s and made a number of locomotives, both themselves and in association with Brush. Production ceased at Stafford after the take-over by English Electric in 1961. The last two built at Stafford were a pair of small but very neat 4 wheelers. Built in 1961 (WB 3207 & 3208) and weighing in at only 16 tons. They were fitted with a 5cyl Gardner 5LW engine of 90bhp driving through a British Twin Disc transmission to a Wiseman reversing and reduction gearbox fitted to the rear axle. They were both ordered by Leys Malleable Castings, one for the Derby factory and one for an associated firm in Lincoln. (WB No 3207 of 1961) and is seen here at the Foxfield Railway in Staffordshire Sept 1994.

Two locomotives ordered by the CEGB to the Bagnall design after the take-over by English Electric 1961 were transferred to the Robert Stephenson works in Darlington for erection. They were nam Hengist and Horsa and unusually for industrial locos were fitted with vacuum train brakes from new. Th have a Dorman 6QA engine of 262bhp driving through a Twin-Disc hydraulic transmission. They wei in at 40 tons and departed from the normal Bagnall design in that the final drive was fitted directly o the rear axle, rather that having a jackshaft. *Above.* GET No2 (RSH No 8368/WB No 3213 of 1962) v named Horsa and went to Richborough power station in Kent and then to Bedford power station. Its cla to fame was as a star in the James Bond film Octopussey. It is seen on the Mid-Norfolk Railway at Cou School in 1994.

Left.
Hengist (RSH 8367/ WB 3212 of 1968) later worked for English China Clay at Quidhampton and is seen shunting tank wagons along what was the old GWR line from Salisbury to Westbury in November 1990.

E.E. Baguley of Burton on Trent were early pioneers in the use of internal combustion engines for railway transport. They are still in business today, but not building locomotives.

Right. Baguley-Drewry 4 wheel (BD 3733 of 1977) is seen on the Mid-Norfolk Railway as GET No in 2001. These relatively modern small locos were built for the MoD and this one worked for the Navy at Gosport. It only weighed 15 tons and is fitted with Perkins 162bhp V8 engine driving through a Twin-Disc transmission to give 12,000lbs tractive effort.

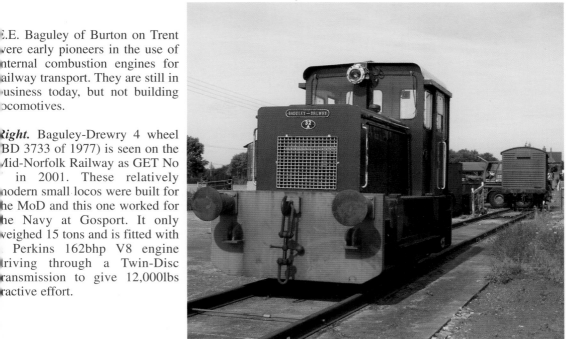

Andrew Barclay of Kilmarnock was established in the mid 1800s and is also still in business. *Below.* 0-4-0 DM (AB 371 of 1945) marked up as Army 235 at the Isle of Wight Steam Railway, Haven Street depot in 2005. It was built for the army in 1945 to their standard design with Gardner 150bhp engine and a Wilson SCG gearbox, giving a tractive effort of 11,760lbs. It was originally allocated to Bicester but also served at Eskmeal in Cumbria, Morton-on-Lugg in Herefordshire and Long Marston in Warwickshire, before going to its present home.

A pair of Andrew Barclay's 0-4-0 diesel hydraulics (AB 578 & 579 of 1972) were built for the MoD and worked at the Royal Ordnance factory at Puriton near Bridgewater. After the rail connection to the factory was disconnected in 1994, the pair were transferred to the West Somerset Railway to work PW trains. They were built to work as a pair and the inter-loco couplings can be clearly seen on 578 (*right*) at the Dunster PW depot. They have 302hp Paxman 6RPHL Mk7 engines and weigh 35 tons.
Photos by Malcolm Best,
www.preservedshunters.co.uk
And Graham Turner
www.railblue.com
Information,
Paul Conibeare WSR.

Above. Barclay 0-6-0DH (AB 510 of 1966) at Queenborough Wharf on the Isle of Sheppey. It is seen in April 2006, unloading imported steel and transporting it to the plant which is about a mile away. The four locos that work this branch line were originally built for the MoD and used in Germany by the BAOR. They are fitted with a 6cyl Cummings engine.

Below. Seen at the Rutland Railway Museum in April 2006. This diesel mechanical (AB 415 of 1957) has a Cummings 6cyl engine of 400bhp, with a weight of about 42 tons. It originally worked for the CEGB at Castle Donnington Power Station.

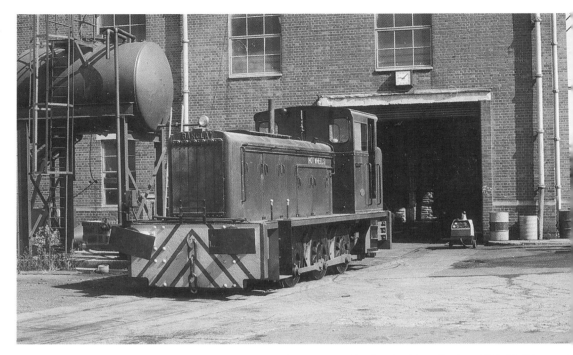

Above. Barclay 0-6-0 (AB 422 of 1958) named "HOTWHEELS", fitted with a Gardner 8L3 204bhp engi̶
and mechanical transmission to give 15,600 TE. It was built for the CEGB and used at Swansea, Bidefc̶
and Reading. It is shown in July 1985 at the old Northampton Power Station. It was used at the time a̶
grain store and the locomotive had just been started in readiness to collect a grain wagon from a BR lo̶
Below. Westoe Colliery was once part of the Harton Coal Co, situated on the coast at South Shields. A li̶
to the coal staithes on the River Tyne, where this Barclay would hand over to the electric locomotive ̶
the unloading into the ships. The 0-4-0DH (AB 623) stands with the North Sea as a backdrop in Mar̶
1989.

Brush Traction of Loughborough built their first diesel in 1939 and are still in the locomotive business today. **Above.** They built four 0-6-0 DE shunters for the new Tyne & Wear Metro system in 1978, numbered WL1 to 4 with a Rolls Royce DV8N engine of 427bhp. Seen here is No WL4 (B 804) at the Gosford shed, it now resides at the Rutland Railway Museum. ***Photos by Jerry Glover and www.rail-photos.com***
Below. A Brush locomotive but built by Brush-Beyer-Peacock at Gorton in 1958 for the Steel Company of Wales. This was the first of a number of similar locos and was allocated both a Brush and a Beyer-Peacock works number (No B91/BP 7856). It is fitted with a National Gas 220bhp engine driving through Brush traction motors giving 19,200lbs tractive effort. It weighs 30 tons and has a speed of 18 mph. It can be seen at the Middleton Railway in Leeds.

Very few new shunters have been built in the UK in recent years (as apposed to refurbished), but Clay[Equipment received an order for two such locomotives in 2000 for use in the Royal Navy Devonp Dockyard. Clayton were part of the Rolls Royce group until a recent management buy out. Their fact at Hatton near Derby manufactures mainly narrow gauge mining locomotives, but also has the ability to produce standard gauge. *Above*. These locomotives (No B4314 A & B) are powered by a 6 cyl Deutz BF6M1013E diesel engine through a Clarke hydraulic transmission to a Clayton axle mounted spur and bevel final drive. Weight is 25 tons and they have a tractive effort of approx 6,725kg. Notice the two sets of buffers. *Below*. An older locomotive supplied to the MoD at Rosyth, was a 4wDH (CE B1840 of 1979), seen in the works when new. It is fitted with a Perkins 95bhp 6.354 engine.

Inset. At its present location on the Keith & Dufftown Railway.
Photo, Roy Etherington. Information and main photographs kindly supplied by Clayton Equipment L with help from Bob Darvill of IRS.

he Drewry Car Co of London was a name associated with shunting locomotives especially for BR, but ey were never a manufacturer, only a design and sales company. Building was carried out by such as the ulcan Foundry and Robert Stephenson Hawthorns, as with the BR class 04 or under licence as in the case f the class 03. They also produced many smaller versions for industry. The smaller locos had 4 wheels stead of 6, a 6cyl Gardner L3 153bhp engine instead of a 8cyl, 4 speed Wilson transmission instead of a speed and only weighed 23 tons instead of 28 tons.

bove. GET No3 (RSH7922/DC 2589 of 1957) is seen at the northern end of the Mid-Norfolk Railway at ounty School in 1994. This loco was originally new to Dover Gas Works and then to Purfleet Deep Wharf d now resides at the Barrow Hill Roundhouse near Chesterfield. It can be regularly seen moving steam gines on the turntable and carries the name 'HARRY'.

elow. A Vulcan Foundry built example (VF D293/DC 2566 of 1955) looking very smart at Epping & ngar Railway in Essex, October 2005. It also worked for many years on the south side of the Thames at rith Wharf before going to Norfolk as GET No5. It is now named "HEATHER" with the Number D1995. *hoto by David Tutton & www.rail-photos.com*

Above. Seeing industrial shunters on the main line is unusual, but on the 3rd of August 1982 GEC/Engl
Electric 0-6-0DH (EEV 3870 of 1969) is seen at Billingham, having been turned on the triangle at Nort
It had a 274bhp Dorman engine and was owned by BASF at Seal Sands. This locomotive was built at
Vulcan Foundry, which was by 1969 owned by GEC, but still using the English Electric name and the
name badge on the front radiator grill. This loco is now on the Weardale Railway in Co Durham.
Photo, Jerry Glover and www.preservedshunters.co.uk

Below. The remains of Wissington Light Railway were still in use in 1974, as was the stub of the G
Stoke Ferry branch. They were used to serve the large British Sugar Corporation factory at Wissington
Norfolk. English Electric 0-4-0DH (EEV D1123 of 1966) is seen shortly after leaving the old Abb
Station and crossing the Black Drain on it way to the factory. This loco is now at the Nene Valley railw

Many early firms used dummy steam chimneys, including Fowler of Leeds.

Above. This 0-4-0DM (JF 4100003 of 1946) was originally from Croda Hydrocarbons of Rotherham where it was named "H.W.ROBINSON", it is seen shunting at Emsay Railway in West Yorkshire. It is fitted with 80hp engine, (probably Fowler-Saunders) through a fowler mechanical gearbox. Notice the jackshaft drive is at the front of the locomotive indicating that the engine and gearbox assembly is fitted the opposite way to many other makes. This is now (2006) undergoing full restoration and repainting.
Photo by Charles Adams and supplied by the Embsay & Bolton Abbey Steam Railway.
Below. An area once in the headlines as a result of a high speed crash is Great Heck in Yorkshire. Fowler 0-4-0DH (JF 4220038 of 1966) stands on the short branch at the Plasmor concrete block factory 30th March 2005. This loco is fitted with 203bhp Leyland Albion engine and was delivered new to Thornhill Power Station in Dewsbury. After spending some time at the Middeton Railway it arrived at Great Heck in 1993. *Photo, Wilson R Adams and rail-photos.com. Information by Gary Kaye, Plasmor.*

Above. A wet day in Milford Haven in October 1980 as Fow 0-4-0DM (JF 4200016 of 1947) brings the daily fish tra towards the station and a waiting class 37 loco, for onwa shipment. At this time there were extensive sidings around t docks and a connection into the Naval Armaments depot. T Station is behind the camera and still remains today, but with sidings.

Below. GEC Traction (new name after the amalgamation English Electric & AEI in 1972) received an order in the m 1970s from the then British Steel Co, for a small fleet of locos the blast furnaces at Scunthorpe. A fleet of seven were built und licence by Baguley, known as the highline locos and used

supply coke and iron ore to t furnaces. Because of their dut they are rarely seen in t condition of No HL2 (GEC 5435/BD3735 of 1977). Fitt with a 6cyl Rolls Roy supercharged engine and GE traction motor, weighing 26 to with 7,200kg of tractive effe One interesting point about the vehicles is that the drivi controls are fitted to the rear w of the cab as they were designed work in tandem with others in t fleet.

Main photo by
the Appleby Frodingham
Railway Preservation Society.

Above. GEC 6w diesel electric locomotive No 272 named "GROSMONT" (GECT No 5470 of 1978) at the Corus quarry at Shap near Penrith. A number of these locomotives were built in the late seventies for British Steel, all have Dorman 12QT 650 or 760bhp engine, electric transmission and they weigh in at between 76 & 80 tons. *Below.* Another later locomotive from GEC (GEC 5578 of 1980) is seen at the Rugby cement works in Cambridgeshire in 2005. This is possibly the last standard gauge locomotive built under the GEC name and the last one at the Vulcan Foundry. The loco behind is a 4w Thomas Hill (TH 178v of 1967).

F C Hibberd built Planet locomotives were found at work in many small yards across the country. The[ ]
normally weighed about 23 tons and could be fitted with a Dorman, Leyland or Foden engines.

Above. Seen at British Industrial Sand plant, on the stub of the closed line from Kings Lynn to Dereha[m]
in August 1977 is No3 (FH 3678 of 1953).

Below. A Planet 4wDM is seen at the Vaynor quarry, Machen, South Wales in April 1986. This quarry s[till]
survives as a stub from Newport on the old Brecon & Merthyr/GWR line to Bedwas. It (FH 3832 of 195[ ])
was built new for Dorman Long in Middlesborough and passed through a number of owners includi[ng]
British Industrial Sand at Redhill. It weighs 23 tons and is fitted with a 117bhp Dorman engine and is n[ow]
at the Bideford Railway Station in Devon, hauling passenger trains.

Above. Planet 4wDM (FH 3491 of 1951) at the Rom River depot in Witham Essex in 1977. This was part of the closed Maldon to Witham branch line and was left in place for a few years just to serve this site.

Below. This was one of the first diesel locomotives built by the famous Leeds firm of Hunslet (HE 1697 of 1932) and was tried out by the main line companies in the 1930s. It was originally owned by the LMS and then by the War Dept before returning to Hunslet after the war for rebuilding. The original MAN engine was replaced with a 132bhp McLaren Ricardo engine and used as a works shunter. It was obtained by the Middleton railway in 1960 where it can be seen today in its original LMS livery.

Above. An early Hunslet at the Threlkeld Quarry & Mining Museum in Cumbria in 1987 (HE 2389 1941). The MoD purchased a number of this type of loco in 1940 for various ammunition depots, they h special features fitted to prevent sparks and were fitted with Gardner engines and mechanical transmissic *Below.* A diesel at the steam Didcot Railway Centre, Hunslet 0-6-0DM DL26 (HE 5238 of 1962). This lc is fitted with 264bhp National engine and the Hunslet mechanical gearbox, that utilises a heavy fc operated clutch.

bove. This gives some idea of the quality of the track Industrials have to traverse. Hunslet 0-6-0DH (HE 685 of 1968) named "BIG JOHN", heads towards the private quay at Queenborough in Kent May 1994. This locomotive (now scrapped) was fitted with a Rolls Royce 8cyl supercharged engine and Twin Disc transmission . Below. A fleet of 11 big Bo-Bo Hunslets was built in 1972/3 for British Steel Corporation now Corus) for their Scunthorpe steel works and are still running there today. They were unusual for Hunslet in being a diesel electric (as required by BSC) and all travelled from Leeds by rail when new. They re powered by 2 x Rolls Royce V8 engines to give 1124 bhp, driving through Brush electrical equipment. Veight is 90 tons and have been converted to remote control.

Below. No 75 (HE 7286 of 1972) shown in the steelworks.

Photo by Bryan Dawes.

Hudswell Clarke of Leeds was a large producer of industrial locomotives trading under the name of t
Railway Foundry. *Above*. Powell Duffryn Fuels Ltd 0-6-0 DM (HC D1253 of 1962) at Dibles Wha
Southampton in March 1986. This was originally a Manchester Ship Canal Co locomotive numbered D
It was fitted with a Gardner 8L3 8cyl engine of 204bhp driving through a S.S.S Powerflow gearbox a
jackshaft. It developed 16,500lbs tractive effort and weighed 36 tons.

Below. One very attractive location for industrial locomotive is the branch line from Ashdon Gate
Wapping Wharf in Bristol. This line is now part of the Bristol Harbour Railway but before that it was us
to bring in household coal to the Western Fuel Co depot. Hudswell Clarke 0-6-0DM named "WESTEF
PRIDE" (HC D1171 of 1959) is seen alongside the River Avon on the 19th April 1985 with eight load
coal wagons.

Above. Two of the largest diesel locomotives supplied to the Manchester Ship Canal were two 0-6-0 diesel electrics from Hudswell Clarke, seen here on the East Lancashire Railway in July 2003. No 4002 (HC D1076 of 1959) is paired with an ex BR class 08. These fine machines were fitted with a National Gas cyl engines of 400bhp driving through Brush electrical equipment to give 34,000lbs of tractive effort and top speed of 18 mph. Note by the photograph the difference in drivers visibility between the BR standard class 08 shunter and a similar one supplied for industry. Photo by Andrew Mitchell.

Below. Hudswell Clarke (HC D1373 of 1965) at the Esso site in Plymouth. This was one of a batch of four locomotives ordered originally for the Mersey Docks & Harbour Board. It weighs 36 tons, has a Gardner L3B engine and drives through a British Twin Disc transmission to give 23,400lbs of tractive effort.

North British were better known for their main line locos in the UK and world markets, but also built ma[ny]
industrial shunters. *Above.* "CORONATION", 0-4-0 DH (NB 27097 of 1953) is seen at the Foxfi[eld]
railway in September 1994. It has a Paxman 6cyl VEE RPHX engine, Voith transmission and weighs [...]
tons. *Below.* Another North British product is seen working in the Mayer Parry scrap yard at Snailwell n[ear]
Newmarket (a final resting place of so many diesels) in November 1990. It is a 275bhp 0-4-0DH (276[...]
of 1958) and was originally used by the Army at Bicester and was still carrying its MoD No 410.

Left. Built, and now working in Scotland, is this Mk1 design North British shunter, 0-4-0 DH (NBL 27415 of 1954). Originally owned by Esso Petroleum at Fawey. It then spent some time at the Isle of Wight Railway before going to its present home at the SRPS Bo'ness. It has a 275bhp Paxman V6RPH engine and NBL/Voith transmission, to give 22,850lbs of tractive effort. Weighing 34 tons with a top speed of 15 mph (a standard speed for most shunting locomotives).
Information by Kevin A McCallum and photo by Andrew Mitchell.

Below. The famous chocolate firm of Cadburys had a railway system in their yard at Bournville near Birmingham. When they changed from steam to diesel operation, they purchased a fleet of four very neat locos from the North British Locomotive Co. Below. No 14 (NBL 28037 of 1961) is seen at the plant, this would have had a MAN engine and Voith/NBL transmission, connecting through a jackshaft drive. These locomotives were built just after an order for 72 similar ones for British Railways. No 14 lasted up until traffic went over to road transport in 1976, then sold to Thomas Ward Ltd and went to Briton Ferry in Glamorgan. ***Photo Rodney Weaver and IRS.***

Above. Peckett & Sons of Bristol were well known for their industrial steam locomotives, but only b᷾
five diesels. Seen here is 200bhp 0-4-0 DM (P5003 of 1958) on the Middleton Railway in Leeds, j᷾
passing under the M1 Motorway and paired with Thomas Hill 4wDH (TH 139C of 1964). It was origina᷾
purchased by James Austin Ltd at Thornhill where it was given the name "AUSTINS No1". The Middlet᷾
claims to be the oldest public railway in the world, being the first to obtain an Act of Parliament in 175᷾
Photo, Andrew Mitchell and www. preservedshunters.co.uk
Below. A large and a modern British built shunting locomotive is RFS 1994 built Co-Co diesel hydrau᷾
named "CRACOE" seen at the Tilcon quarry near Skipton. It has a 503bhp Caterpiller engine and weig᷾
in at 150 tons. The cab shows its decadency from Sentinel, through Rolls Royce and Thomas Hill.

industrial locomotives make ideal maintenance motive power for heritage railways. **Above**. Seen in July 2006 is 0-6-0DH (RR 10187 of 1964) on a ballast train at the restored Stanhope Station in Co Durham. This loco was originally at the NCB Daw Mills Colliery and is now at the recently re-opened Weardale Railway. It weighs in at 48 tons and has a RR 8cyl supercharged engine giving 29,500lbs of tractive effort. The loco on the other end of the train is a English Electric 0-6-0DH. *Photo by Kevin Hilary of the Weardale Railway Trust.*

Below. The area around Buxton in Derbyshire is still an important place for rail freight with a number of lime stone quarries. Buxton Lime Industries of Tunstead has some industrial locomotives including No SCW/1/29 named "DOVEDALE" seen in 1993. This 0-6-0DH (RR 10284 of 1969) was built at Shrewsbury as a standard Sentinel design but rebuilt by Thomas Hill in 1974. Two obvious changes made are the shutter type engine doors and changes to the cab doors, the standard doors being notorious for letting in water and jamming.

Above. One of Rolls Royce's later locomotive designs was the 6w chain drive Steelman class with a RR 608bhp DV82 engine and weighing 60 tons. BSC No 37 (RR 10275 of 1969) is seen at the Gretton Brook shed of British Steel in the last days of operation, May 1980. Also in operation at the site were a number of the ex BR class 14s, one of which (BSC No 52 BR D9537 of 1965) is also seen.

Below. Preston Docks is still handling tanker trains as seen in this photo in 1985 but now controlled by the Ribble Steam Railway. Rolls Royce 4wDH "PROGRESS" (RR 10283 of 1968) is seen in the docks, notice the low height of this particular design.

Ruston & Hornsby of Lincoln made a large amount of shunting locos until taken over by English Electric in 1966. At the smaller end of their standard gauge range were the 48DS and the 88DS types.

Above. Ex Army 4wDM 48DS No110 (RH 411319 of 1953) is seen at the Rutland Railway Museum in 2006. These weighed a mere 7.5 Tons and had a 48bhp Ruston 4cyl VRO engine and a simple mechanical gearbox.

Below. Seen at PD Fuels, Hamworthy Quay in Dorset is 4w class 88DS (RH 242867 of 1946) in June 1976 shunting 16 ton coal wagons. This loco has the Ruston 4PVH 88bhp engine and is one of the 254 of this type built at Lincoln.

Above. Rugby Cement works at Barrington in Cambridgeshire was the last quarry in the UK to work with rail wagons and dragline. Ruston 165DE 0-4-0 No 8 (RH 499436 of 1963) is seen in the quarry in June 1996 with a train of tippler wagons.

Below. A weekend line up of locomotives at Purfleet Deep Wharf in 1991. The line up is from right to left Ruston 165DH 0-4-0 (RH No 457303 of 1963), No 6 Drewry 0-4-0DM (DC2583/VF D297 of 1956), No 5 Drewry 0-4-0 DM (DC 2589/RSH 7922 of 1957), last one is one of the two Ruston LPSH locos on site (RH 512463/4 of 1965).

malgamation of the old established and well known firm of Robert Stephenson, with the locomotive
uilder Hawthorns Leslie & Co Ltd in 1937 became, Robert Stephenson & Hawthorns Ltd, with factories
t Newcastle and Darlington. They were absorbed into English Electric in 1955 and ceased diesel
roduction in 1963. A unique vehicle is this Stephenson Crossley 0-6-0 DM (RSH 7697 of 1953). It was
ne of a number of locos built by the company with engines by Crossleys of Manchester. Three were built
or the Calverton Colliery and this one at the Tanfield Railway is the only one left in its original condition.
: is powered by a Crossley 6cyl engine of 300bhp, driving through a Vulcan-Sinclair fluid coupling to a
iree speed gearbox. Tractive effort is 24,750lbs. It is seen at the Tanfield Railway in Co Durham June
005.

Top photo
Bryan Dawes
www.preservedshunters.co.uk
Lower Photo by
D Hewitt,
Tanfield Railway

Thomas Hill at Kilnhurst near Rotherham was originally a servicing and repair facility for diesel shunters and was taken over by Rolls Royce in 1963. They were also well known from the early 1960s for their conversions of Sentinel steam locomotives into diesels. A rebuild can be distinguished by the letter 'c' after the works number. Eventually Rolls Royce transferred all loco production to Thomas Hill and concentrated diesel engine production at Shrewsbury. They traded under the name of "Vanguard". Seen above is 4wDH (TH 163V of 1966) at the Rugby cement works at Barrington near Cambridge. This locomotive is fitted with a 206bhp 6 cyl RR engine and Twin Disc hydraulic transmission to give 20,000lbsTE. It is seen here in 2005 in use at the quarry shortly before this part of the production changed over to mechanical dumper operation. It is now GET 10 at the Bressingham Steam Museum in Norfolk.

Left.
One of the Thomas Hill built Sentinel designs is seen at the exchange sidings of Castle Cement plant near Stamford
(TH 293V of 1980) .

Photo Bryan Dawes.

The Mendip Hills in Somerset are important for rail-borne stone traffic, with two large quarries near Frome.

Above. An unidentified Thomas Hill Vanguard 0-6-0 design is seen shunting at Hansons, Whatley Quarry in November 1987. These locomotives were built in the 1970s and were equipped with Rolls Royce engines of 272, 350 or 400bhp driving through SCG transmission.

Below. Another Thomas Hill Vanguard is seen on the Bicester Military Railway in August 1996. The railway that serves the very large depot is in two distinct areas of Graven Hill and Arncott with a branch line between the two. Photographers are not encouraged but one section is in open country with a level crossing and once a platform for passenger trains. These 4-wheeled diesel hydraulics are now the mainstay of the MoD fleet and have recently been overhauled with their Rolls Royce engine changed for a Cummings unit.

Above. Army No 263 (TH 303V of 1982) from the nearby Ludgershall base adjacent to the Salisbury Battle Area, is seen at Andover Station during an open day in March 1986. It is on show with a train of military vehicles as GWR 4930 "HAGLEY HALL" leaves the Station.

Below. Rugby Cement 4wDH No 9 (TH 186v of 1967) entering the Barrington works with a empty cement train of Pressflow wagons in 1978. The works is at the end of a short branch line near Cambridge containing three level crossings and a concrete viaduct to connect to BR.

Rebuilds are now becoming popular with a number of firms provide this service, including RMS Locotec and HNRC. One firm that rebuilt a number of industrial shunters in the 1990s was the renamed, Yorkshire Engine Co, based in Rotherham. Here we see two locomotives that have changed their appearance since being built at Leeds and Shrewsbury. *Above.* Ex Hunslet 0-4-0DH (originally HE 9225 of 1984 now YEC L143). Originally built for the BAOR with Rolls Royce 300bhp engine, but now rebuilt with a Caterpillar 3406 series 440bhp unit. *Below.* Ex Sentinel 0-4-0 DH (originally S 10128 of 1963 now YEC L142) This locomotive would originally have had a Rolls Royce engine, but now has a Perkins 2006 series 354bhp unit. This company was not connected with the original Yorkshire Engine Company of Rotherham which closed in 1965. Both locomotives are seen at the Old Dalby test track in Leicestershire in 2001 and 2004 where they were being used to shunt stock including the new Virgin Pendalino. *Photos by Bryan Dawes.*

The Yorkshire Engine Co based at Meadowhall, Sheffield were the main supplier to the steel industry. After being taken over by United Steel in 1948 they produced their first diesel locomotive in 1950.

Over the coming years they built up a fine reputation with their diesel electric designs, using mainly Rolls Royce engines. They produced many double ended locomotives including the well known Janus. Called Janus, from the "God of the Gates and Doors" in Roman mythology, having the ability to look both backwards and forwards at the same time. They were fitted with two Rolls Royce C6SFL engines with a combined power of 440 bhp, giving a tractive effort of 32,000lbs. These highly regarded locos were fitted with a centre cab (looking the same at the front as the back) and weighed in at 48 tons. with a speed of 2? mph.

Above. Scunthorpe's No 90 (YE2943 of 1965) stands for the camera with a new coat of paint.
Photo from Appleby Frodingham Railway Preservation Society.
Top right. An unidentified Janus shunts at the Bromford Works of the British steel Corporation in June 1994 just prior to its closure.
Below. One of the Janus type, No 37 is seen at Flixborough Wharf near Scunthorpe in September 198? (YE 2738 of 1959).

Yorkshire Engine Co also produced many single engine types including the class 02 for British Railways. *Above.* 0-6-0 DE (YE 2745 of 1960) is the centre of attention at the South Devon Railway in June 2005. These were fitted with a RR 6cyl 200bhp engines, BTH electrical gear and weight of 30 tons. *Photo by David Tutton.*

Below. Corus has a plant at Workington in Cumbria for the production of rails, although this is soon to be relocated to Scunthorpe. Here 0-6-0DH No 309 (YE 2825 of 1961) is seen with the Irish Sea as a backdrop in June 1997.

Left.
Owned by Allied Wire & Steels Co this single ended Yorkshire No 37("CARLISLE" (YE 2755 of 1959) i photographed during a Branch Lin Society's tour of Cardiff Docks i Sept 1987. Much of the nearby are where this photo was taken has no been re-developed into the Cardif Bay development.

Below.
Yorkshire Engine Co built some larg 0-8-0s in the 1960s, called Indus an Taurus. The latter type went to Britis Railways and two of the Indus typ went to the steelworks. They were 6(tons in weight with two Rolls Royc C8SFL engines giving a total o 600bhp and a massive 44,000lbs o tractive effort. The one seen below i (YE 2894 of 1962) at the Corby stee works in May 1982 just as most of th internal system was closing.

The Appleby Frodingham Railway Preservation Society held a diesel day at the giant Corus Scunthorpe Steel plant on the 29th & 30th of March 2006. A number of locomotives, not normally seen in public were on view and taking people around the plant. It has many miles of track and a fleet of over 30 locomotives operating around the clock. *Below.* The Society's own diesel, Yorkshire 0-6-0DE (YE2661 of 1958) was used on one tour and is seen awaiting its turn and later crossing a road within the plant. Notice the emblems, including the shire horse, BTH electrical badge, name, makers, Railway Executive plates and the plate on the battery box giving the addresses of engine, electrical and loco makers. It is painted in the colours of the Eccles Slag Co who originally operated on the site.

One of the previously described Highline Locos, also took a turn with passenger trains and here seen near the station.
It is 0-4-0DE No4 (GETC 5437/BD 3737 of 1977).

Above. One of the large Bo-BoDE Hunslets No 75 (HE 7286 of 1972) was also used and is seen heading from the station back to the depot. The main duties of these locomotives is to use their 58,000lbs of tractive effort hauling 550 ton molten metal torpedo wagons from the blast furnace to the steel making plant.
Inset. Preserved within the site is a slag ladle wagon used until the 1980s to dump the slag, the glow of this could be seen for miles around. *Below.* One of the remaining Yorkshire Janus locomotives, No1 (YE 2877 of 1963). These have been the main motive power at the plant for over 40 years and on the day of the tour, four were in operation at the Anchor Sidings. Many of both these type have now been fitted with remote control, which at times can give the impression that the locomotives are moving without any control. *Photo by J Edgar.*

The British Sugar Corporation were good customers of Ruston & Hornsby of Lincoln. They operated about eighteen factories, mainly in the east of the country and had an unusual operating requirement. For most of the summer months the factories were effectively closed, but during the winter months they were working 24/7. In the early days most of the sugar beet came in by rail from the surrounding Stations and the finished sugar or cattle feed went out by rail. By the 1950s, just as the diesels were starting to be delivered much of the traffic was starting to go over to road transport, especially the beet.

Above. The favoured type for BSC was the Ruston DS type as seen (RH 310088 of 1951) at Ipswich in August 1974. The DS type was fitted with a rather large Ruston 6VPH engine of 165bhp which was started by the use of a donkey engine. This is a small hand-start petrol engine fitted with a 150psi compressor. This small hand start engine would be started and build up air pressure in a receiver until there was enough to start the main engine. The locos weighed 28 tons for the 0-4-0 wheel version and 30 tons for the 0-6-0s but the power output was very similar. *Below.* The Ipswich factory had a shunting yard next to the GE main line (seen on the right) and the last Ruston purchased by the BSC (second hand from dealer Thomas Wards) is seen shunting here on the 2nd Nov 1974. The locomotive is a 0-4-0DE type 165DE (RH 408304 of 1957) and has a 165bhp Ruston 6VPH engine driving a AEI generator and traction motor with a weight of 28 tons.

Above. Cantley in Norfolk is in an exposed position near the River Yare but next to the line to Yarmouth and Lowestoft. Rail traffic had ended when this photo was taken on the 29th March 1990, as can be seen by the state of some of the wagons. The only working locomotive Ruston 0-6-0DM type 165DS (RH 304468 of 1950) shunts some redundant wagons and the other loco (RH 395301 of 1956) past the main line. Note the Cantley signal box in the distance.

Below. Kings Lynn's Ruston 0-4-0DM, a 165DS type (RH 327974 of 1954) is seen shunting oil tanks into the factory in Oct 1989. The track in the foreground and in the background is the old M&GN line from South Lynn to the Midlands.

Workington also has a working port with a rail system that connects the steel plant to Network Rail.
Above. 25th Sept 2006, a few weeks after the steel plant closed, Hunslet 0-6-0DH No2 (HE 8977 of 1979) was busy transporting rails from the docks to the plant for final finishing. It is seen crossing the River Derwent on a concrete bridge towards an interchange siding on the side of the Irish Sea. This is one of the four locomotives owned by the port and is fitted with a Cummings NTA855 engine of 388bhp and weighs 0 tons.
Below. Later a Corus 0-6-0DH Hunslet No403 (HE 7543 of 1978) is seen hauling the train along the short branch to the works.

Thanks to Alan Graham of the Port of Workington for help and information.

The National Coal Board was a major user of industrial locomotives, both for surface and underground operation. Obviously the company was reluctant to change to diesel operation for its surface locos, but by the 1970s had nearly 500 standard gauge diesels, along with some hundreds of steam, narrow gauge and electrics. The company was divided into many areas and executives covering the whole country, each with its own buying policies. For this reason, and the fact that they purchased many second hand machines, they had a huge variety of vehicles and manufacturers on their books.

Above. Manton Main Collieries, Hudswell Clarke 0-6-0DM (HC D1121 of 1958) is seen shunting over the main road in March 1977. The wagon next to the loco is one of the many internal user vehicles used by NCB.

Below. Another Hudswell Clarke 0-4-0DM (HC D1094 of 1959) seen at Park Mill Colliery, Clayton West in Yorkshire, August 1980. This low-powered loco had a 72bhp Gardner 4LW engine giving it only 5,740 lbs TE with a weight of only 13 tons. The line in the background is now part of the Kirklees Light railway.

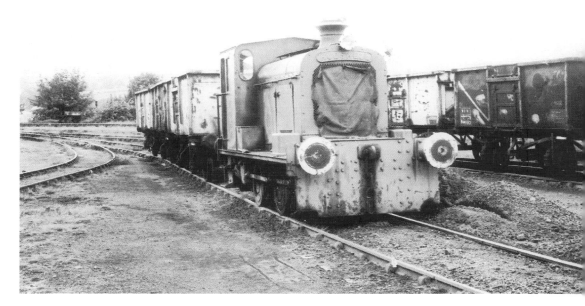

Above. Industrials very often go where other locos dare not. This John Fowler 0-4-0DM (JF No 4200016 of 1947) named "F.B.ROBJENT" looks lost in the docks at Milford Haven in Oct 1980. It is in fact on its way to collect the fish train for transfer from the fish market to the BR station.

Below. Another loco that seems to have lost its way is this 4wDH Thomas Hill (TH 177c of 1967) at the Redland's yard in Norwich, March 1991. The Norwich Bruff re-railing vehicle has just arrived (driven by the Author) to put it back where it should be. Thomas Hill rebuilt a number of Sentinel steam locos into diesels in the 60s and the 'c' after the number indicates that this was originally a vertical boiler steam locomotive (Sentinel No 9401 of 1950).

DIESEL LOCOMOTIVE BUILDERS

During the steam age in the UK there were a wealth of locomotive builders, from small concerns producing only a few locomotive per year to very large companies producing not only for British industry, but for main line companies and for all the World. As firms slowly realised the age of steam was coming to an end they started to change over to diesel manufacture. About a dozen steam builders started to produce diesel locomotives, but by the end of the 1960s few were left. However, as well as the steam builders a number of other firms came to the market including, Ruston, English Electric, Motor Rail and of course Brush, who also are still building and repairing today. The other builder of shunting locomotives was of course British Railways, who had many workshops around the country. Their range of shunters was limited to the well know BR class 08 and the class 03 built under licence, but both types were made in large quantities and in different works. BR did not produce any for industry, just for its own yards. Locomotives built by industry for British Railways differed in a number of small design details, such as the requirement for train brakes and they normally required side entry cabs, industry normally had rear entry. There was a lot of sub contracting between companies with one firm making the bodies and another firm making the electrical parts, so some locomotives came out as Brush/Bagnall, Brush/Beyer, Drewry/Robert Stephenson or Drewry/Vulcan. North British decided to go into collaboration with the Germans and produced a range of locomotives with MAN engines and Voith transmission, but unwisely decided to make many of the items under licence. One builder that stands out from the others is the Lincoln firm of Ruston & Hornsby. They were one of the few firms who built the whole locomotive, including the engine and gearbox and went on to be the largest producer of shunting locomotives in the UK. They were nearly all exclusively built for industry, except a few including the class 07 for BR. By the 1960s there were too many builders chasing a rapidly declining market and many stretched themselves and came crashing down, or had to join forces with larger companies. One firm that swallowed up many was English Electric and in the process became one of the market leaders, until it became GEC then Marconi, before amalgamating with Alstom of France.

Below.
Hunslet Yardmaster (HE 5306 of 1958) pulling out of the original Andrew Barclay factory and crossing West Langlands Street towards the BR connection in 1987. This type of loco is designed to be operated from the ground, the driver is out of site on the other side. Notice the dual gauge track.

A selection of advertisements from the 1950s

51

List of some of the main firms in the UK who built Industrial diesel locomotives.

Associated Equipment Co (AEC) of Southall Middlesex. More famous for building the London bus, bu did build one shunter for its own factory. It boasted the famous bus radiator and is still part of the GWI Societies collection at Southall.

Sir W G Armstrong Whitworth of Newcastle-on-Tyne. A early pioneer of diesel shunters in the 1930s later concentrated on armaments and other MoD work. Produced about 63 units.

Avonside Engine Co of Bristol. An established steam builder who built a small number for industry in th early days.

Andrew Barclay, Sons & Co of Kilmarnock. A firm who concentrated on shunting locomotives, bot steam and diesel. Recently building and repairing main line rail vehicles. Acquired by Hunslet in 1972 an still trading today.

W G Bagnall of Stafford. Built many locomotives under its own name and in collaboration with Brush Became part of English Electric and closed in 1961. The Bagnall design was later taken as the standard E Stephenson range.

Baguley Ltd of Burton-on-Trent. Has a history of building internal combustion locomotives from earl days, with their first diesel in 1929. They built both standard gauge and narrow gauge, mainly for the MoL right up to 1983. The firm is still in existence as Baguley Engineers Ltd, but not building locomotives.

Brush Traction of Loughborough. Better known for its main line products, but in the 50s/60/&70s bui some shunting locomotive, both 4 & 6 wheels and some bogie types. A number of locomotives were bui in collaboration with Bagnalls and Beyer Peacock. One of the few builders still in business.

Beyer Peacock of Gorton, Manchester. A very famous steam locomotive builder who built a number o shunting locomotives in the 1960s in collaboration with other companies before closing in 1966.

Clayton Equipment Co of Hatton in Derby. A firm whose main work is with narrow gauge and minin locomotives, both diesel and battery powered. Has built a few standard gauge shunters and recentl completed two for the Royal Navy.

Drewry Car Co of London. A name is associated with shunters but in fact was only a design company

English Electric. Formed in 1919 and absorbed many builders, most of their products were built a Darlington or the Vulcan Foundry, later became GEC.

GEC of Newton-le-Willows. gained control of AEI and English Electric between 1969 and 1972 , take over by Alstom.

Hudswell Clarke of Leeds. Another large manufacture of shunting locomotives who moved successfull into the diesel age with a number of large orders. Finally taken over by its neighbour, Hunslet Engine C in 1968.

F C Hibbard of Park Royal, London, A builder of small locomotives from the 1930s, both petrol an diesel, ceased production in 1963. They traded under the Planet name. The plant closed in 1964 wit production moving to Derbyshire.

Hunslet Engine Company of Leeds. Perhaps the best known name in shunting locomotives, but als produced main line locomotives, both steam and diesel for the UK and the rest of the world. The compan absorbed many of the other manufacturers over the years but finally closed its doors at the famous Jac Lane works in 1995. The firm stayed in existence and in 2004 started building again at Tamworth i Staffordshire with narrow gauge steam.

John Fowler of Leeds. A well-know builder of small locomotives and traction engines, as well as dies crawler tractors. Ceased production in 1968 and rights passed to Andrew Barclay.

Kerr Stuart of Stoke-on-Trent. One of the first builders of diesel shunting locomotives, but onl produced two standard gauge diesels before being taken over by Hunslet in 1930. One of the locomotive No K4428 was sent to the Hunslet factory for rebuilding and became their first diesel.

Motor Rail of Bedford. A early builder of small internal combustion shunting locomotives for narrow an standard gauge. Ceased production in the mid 1970s. They traded under the Simplex name.

North British Locomotive Co of Glasgow. One of the largest builders of steam locomotives both for th British Railways and for the whole world. They went into diesel production in a big way, building Germa equipment under licence. They were late into the market and were not very successful, going int liquidation in 1963, The rights of the company were acquired by Hunslet.

Peckett of Bristol. A builder of industrial steam locos who turned briefly to diesel production.

Sentinel of Shrewsbury. A well known builder of steam lorries and shunting locomotives. They produced an award-winning design of diesel locomotive. Later taken over by Rolls Royce who moved production to Thomas Hill.

Thomas Hill of Rotherham. Produced Sentinel/Rolls Royce products until production switched to RFS at Doncaster works.

RFS of Doncaster. Formed by a management buyout of part of the BR Doncaster plant in 1988. The remaining Thomas Hill production transferred there in 1993.

Rolls Royce. This well known company purchased Sentinel of Shrewsbury in 1963. They transferred locomotive production to the Thomas Hill factory in 1971, leaving the Shrewsbury site available for diesel engine manufacture.

Ruston & Hornsby of Lincoln. The largest producer of diesel shunters until taken over by English Electric in 1966. The last locomotive leaving the works in 1969. They were one of the few firms to manufacture the whole locomotive.

Robert Stephenson & Hawthorns of Darlington and Newcastle. A direct descendant from the famous firm. Taken over by English Electric and then becoming part of GEC, the last locomotive left the Darlington works in 1963.

Vulcan Foundry of Newton-le-Willows. Taken over by EE and this became their main production base. Locomotive production ceased in 1980 with the site being levelled for redevelopment in about 2003.

Yorkshire Engine Co of Meadowhall, Sheffield. A successful builder of both steam and diesel shunting locomotives, mainly for the steel industry. The firm was owned by British Steel and closed in 1965 with the goodwill passing to Thomas Hill.

The above list shows the vast majority of the industrial diesel shunter builders in the UK, but the Industrial Railway Society's hand book shows over 400 loco builders of all types and some of them will have also built, or re-built the odd diesel loco.

Many locomotives works closed in the 1960s with the equipment being sold or scrapped. ***Below.*** The North British Locomotive Company closed in 1963 and below in a Kettering scrap yard is seen the works shunter from Queens Park Works . This is a more modern type and would have been fitted with a MAN engine and Voith hydraulic transmission.

Makers Plates and Emblems

As industrial locomotives normally have the radiator at the front and most companies would fix their emblem or name here, as was the case in the automotive industry. Possibly one of the best known is the knight and sword of Sentinel (see next page). Sentinel had used a knight as its emblem on its steam road vehicles and this was a carry on. Other firms were English Electric with the rocket, on the Stephenson range. Yorkshire with its Yorkshire grey shire horse and Thomas Hill with the knight on horseback. Most other firms had a large radiator plate with the firms name on, in contrast to main line and BR built shunters. One other area of interest was the maker's plate. On industrial-built locomotives they would give information about the company, its factory, date built, locomotive type, horse power and the number of the unit it was fitted to. In contrast many BR built locomotives simply said, for instance "Built by BR Derby 1966". Some firms also fitted the engine manufacturers plate to the front as was the practice with lorries.

Right.
The front of a MoD Thomas Hill locomotive showing the knight badge on the front and a Rolls Royce engine plate on the side. Most of these locos have recently been overhauled and had their engines replaced with a Cummings unit.

Centre.
The front badge on the North British Locomotives Co Queens Park Works, works shunter, seen in a Kettering scrap yard.

Bottom.
The radiator grill with shire horse emblem seen on a Yorkshire locomotive at Allied Wire & Steel at Cardiff Docks.

Right.
Some locomotives that were required to work on or near the national network, were issued with a plate and number by the British Transport Commission, this one is fitted to a ex NCB Stephenson-range locomotive.

Bottom.
Other emblems fitted were the Stephenson's rocket by English Electric, sword from Sentinel and the knight on horseback from Thomas Hill.

This page.

Yorkshire plates also included the makers of the diesel engine and the manufacturers of the electrical equipment.

The front radiator plate from an early Armstrong Whitworth loco now in the NRMs Locomotion at Shildon.

Photo by Anthony Coulls, NRM.

Two Robert Stephenson plates.

One a diesel that had been built at Newcastle and later plate from a Bagnall locomotive but built at the RSH works at Darlington after the former works had been closed.

An F C Hibberd plate, who called their locos "Planet" and a plate from Hudswell Clarke who always included the words "Railway Foundry".

PRESENT DAY

Today things have changed considerably, with rail freight going out of fashion and the growth of the heritage industry. Things started to change in the 1960s, just as steam was finally disappearing. The combination of the continual transfer of freight onto the roads and the Beeching Axe. This speeded up the closure of many branch lines together with the move away from wagon-load traffic. Consequential to the Beeching cuts, BR found itself with hundreds of relativity new shunters on its hands and decided to sell them on to industry. So over a period of a few years the dozen or so companies who had just geared up to diesel production found themselves with few orders. Some simply shut up shop or sold out to other companies, but a few struggled on with repair work and other forms of manufacture. At this time the new heritage railway market found that many companies were giving away surplus vehicles rather than seeing them cut up. Unfortunately many heritage railways simply used the free traction until it was in need of repair, then scrapped it and looked around for another one. Today (2006) the Heritage railways are the largest owners, with most lines having one or two and some like the Rutland Railway Museum, with as many as 33 on its books, or the Foxfield Railway with 15. There are still a few large users of these locos in industry, with Corus the largest. It has over 30 at Scunthorpe, including a number of the Bo-Bo Hunslets and even some electrics, Teesside has about 30 with a fleet made up of 1977 built large GEC 6w locos. Other users are the MoD with a fleet of recently refurbished 4 wheel Thomas Hills and even British Nuclear Fuels with a fleet of 0-4-0 Hunslets, for moving the waste trains in their Sellafield plant. Also a few small companies have come into the repair and overhaul market. Not strictly builders but rebuilding older vehicles to give them a new identity and a new lease of life. Firms such as Harry Needle Railroad Co working out of Barrow Hill, RMS Locotec of Wakefield and the New Hunslet Engine Co. It's strange that despite the large amount of these vehicles and the amount of heritage railways and museums in the UK there is no designated museum to industrial standard gauge diesels.

Above. Life in preservation for Hunslet GET No 4 (HE 6975 of 1968) at the Bressingham Steam Museum in Norfolk. It is seen loading LMS 2-6-4T No 2500 for transport back to the National Railway Museum at York. Fitted with a 6cyl Rolls Royce engine supplying 17,000 lbs of tractive effort. It was originally purchased by the MoD for Chatham Dockyard and has since been rebuilt by Harry Needle Railroad Co and now works at BNFL plant at Sellafield in Cumbria.

Back page.
Top. A Sentinel design 0-4-0 is seen working along the short branch between the main line and the Castle Cement Works at Ketton, Rutland.
Bottom. The Nene Valley Railway in March 2006 with (left to right) 0-4-0DH (RR 10206 of 1964), Thomas Hill 4wDH (TH 134C of 1964) named "BIRCH COPPICE" and just visible ex London Transport DL83 0-6-0DH Rolls Royce (RR 10271 of 1967).

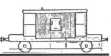